Superpower

Kindness, Friendship, and Empathy

Copyright Elizabeth Devis, 2021 - All rights reserved © The content contained within this book may not be reproduced, duplicated, or transmitted without direct written permission from the author or the publisher. Under no circumstances will any blame or legal responsibility be held against the publisher, or author, for any damages, reparation, or monetary loss due to the information contained within this book. Either directly or indirectly. You are responsible for your own choices, actions, and results.

Legal Notice: This book is copyright protected. This book is for personal use only. You cannot amend, distribute, sell, use, quote, or paraphrase any part, or the content within this book, "Superpower of Kindness, Friendship and Empathy" without the consent of the author or publisher.   Elizabeth Devis.

A note for parents, educators, family members, counselors, coaches, librarians, and other adults:

Dear Adults: Our society currently needs creative people, capable of attaining active goals, diverse thinking, finding both original and non-standard solutions to life's problems, as well as those who can provide their thoughts compassionately, critically, competently, and empathetically.

Your children's social and emotional development plays a giant role in their abilities to achieve success in real life. Social skills are paramount for successfully and effectively interacting with people, collaborating in different groups, achieving goals, reaching a consensus, and resolving conflicts cooperatively with other people.

Developing social skills in your children is imperative for adults. Some children are naturally more socially adept than others. For others, socialization can last throughout a person's life.

In short, this book will help you to manage your child's emotions and behaviors using some easy tips and creative tricks use to strengthen their social skills, be kinder, and make many friends.

A note to a reader

Hello, my friend. Did you know that kindness, empathy, and friendship are some of the most powerful words in your life? But what do friendship and kindness mean to you?

Friendship is devotion, emotional attachment, trust, disinterested communication, sympathy, and empathy, a willingness to help and support each other in difficult times, and a sacrifice for the sake of another person. This is the presence of common interests and values, as well as friendly criticism that helps to walk in another person's shoes.

Kindness is the desire to please others and to perform actions that cause joy, gratitude, and other positive feelings in others. It also involves responsiveness, compassion, and tolerance.

Did you notice that some children communicate and play easily, so they can find and sustain friends everywhere? However, it's a big problem for some other children. If you also have some issues with these character traits, then – this book will help you tremendously.

In this book, you'll discover different situations described to model relationships and behaviors between kids. This resource also offers insight about what you can do in those situations, how to negotiate with people, and how to resolve conflict situations. This book will help you to raise a superhero in you.

So let's start our journey into the wonderful world of friendship, empathy, and kindness.

Kindness and friendship start with a smile.

Kindness and friendship are the best ways to communicate and find new friends.

Kindness is taking care of someone.

If you take care of someone, he or she could be the best friend for you.

Calmness is the cradle of power.

J.G. Holland

Say 'sorry' when you've hurt, teased someone, or made something wrong.

It's never too late to say 'sorry.'

Saying 'please' when you ask something, or 'thank you' after you receive it are the easiest ways to become kind.

'Please' and 'thank you'
are still magic words.

Kindness means
helping people
with special needs.

The best gift you can give a child with special needs is your friendship.

Sharing is being kind.

Sometimes real superheroes live in the hearts of small children.

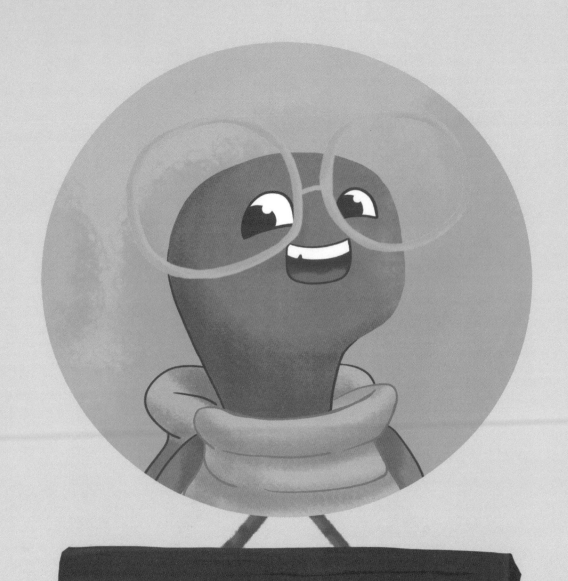

Helping the elderly
doesn't have to be hard.

Older people can be your
good friends, too.

Helping parents with little ones shines the act of kindness.

Brothers and sisters should be as close as hands and feet.

Set your heart on doing good.

Kindness is to praise someone and cheer him or her up.

make kindness a lifestyle.

Friendship is
when you invite friends
to your house.

Friendship is when your friends come over to your house.

Kindness
is when you bring flowers
to your neighbor or teacher.

Flowers can make people happy.

In the end bullies never win.

Create a kindness jar for your friends.

The smallest acts of kindness
can make the biggest impact.

Doing acts activities of kindness
proves the best way
to become a better person.

50 examples of daily acts of kindness

1. Help your family with dinner.

2. Thank a friend with a gift.

3. Compliment 5 people today.

4. Use only positive words.

5. Share a smile with someone.

6. Include a new friend.

7. Write a "thank you" note.

8. Fill a box with toys to donate.

9. Donate used books to someone who needs it.

10. Give someone a compliment.

11. Say "thank you" to someone you don't know.

12. Call and talk to older relatives or grandparents.

13. Catch up with an old friend.

14. Offer help to someone who needs it.

15. Fill up a donation jar.

16. Teach your friend a kindness lesson.

17. Compliment someone's work.

18. Help someone struggling with homework.

19. Hold the door for a stranger.

20. Give an extra hug to your parents.

21. Thank everyone you meet today.

22. Teach someone something new.

23. Help children with special needs.

24. Share your toys/things with friends.

25. Read books about kindness.

26. Brainstorm ideas as a class or with your peers and family.

27. Help family members carry the groceries inside.

28. Clean after your siblings or help parents with cleaning the house.

29. Don't lie and tell the truth to every person you meet.

30. Dedicate 24 hours to spreading positivity.

31. Give flowers to a teacher/neighbor/friend/mom.

32. Leave positive sticky notes in the classroom.

33. Invite someone to play with you on the playground.

34. Feed the birds.

35. Tell a joke or a funny story.

36. Give a candy bar to a first responder, janitor, or a bus driver.

37. Collect money for your favorite charity.

38. Donate any outgrown clothes.

39. Give a lottery ticket to a stranger.

40. Bake cookies for nurses, doctors, police officers, or firefighters.

41. Let someone go ahead of you while waiting in line.

42. Tell your mom or dad how much you love them.

43. Send a postcard to a friend you haven't seen for a long time.

44. Ask for donations instead of birthday gifts.

45. Write a poem and read it to a family member or a friend.

46. Bring dinner to someone.

47. Serve food and water for the homeless.

48. Wash someone's car.

49. Do a favor without asking anything in return.

50. Make someone else's bed.

Here you can write kindness activities which aren't in the list but one that you're eager to try.

Now it's time to start a new *really good habit.*
Commit to doing at least **ONE** (you could make more)
daily kindness each day over the month.
The examples of acts of kindness are written above.
Write the number of the act
of kindness you've performed each day.

How many acts of kindness can you do this month?

30 Days Kindness Challenge

day 1	day 2	day 3	day 4	day 5
day 6	day 7	day 8	day 9	day 10
day 11	day 12	day 13	day 14	day 15
day 16	day 17	day 18	day 19	day 20
day 21	day 22	day 23	day 24	day 25
day 26	day 27	day 28	day 29	day 30

A few words from the author.

Did you know that the main (and the first) source of a child's communicative experience is his or her family, which is a "guide" to the world of knowledge, values, traditions, and experience of modern society? It is from parents that you can learn the rules for communicating with peers, learn to communicate freely. A positive, socio-psychological climate in the family, a warm home atmosphere of love, trust and mutual understanding will help the baby adapt to life and to feel more confident. Specifically, your close relationship with your child will help develop important social skills. Encouraging your child's social–emotional development through warm and loving interactions not only brings you closer to your child, it helps him or her to build skills to achieve success.

If you enjoy this book and found the information in the book helpful, please leave your honest review. You can do it by following the "write a review" button. I'd really appreciate it and will personally read all feedback.

Thank You for Your support.

Printed in Great Britain
by Amazon

14807489R00025